AF380116

# Voices from the Sea

An anthology of poems
by contemporary writers
from Shanghai

Better Link Press

This book is edited and designed by the Editorial Committee of *Cultural China* series

Managing Directors: Wang Youbu, Xu Naiqing
Editorial Director: Wu Ying
Executive Editor: Wu Ying

Compiled by Shanghai Writers Association
Translation by Yawtsong Lee and Sam Meekings

Interior and Cover Design: Yuan Yinchang, Xia Wei

ISBN: 978-1-60220-205-4

Address any comments about *Voices from the Sea*:
*An anthology of poems by contemporary writers from Shanghai* to:

Better Link Press
99 Park Ave
New York, NY 10016
USA
or
Shanghai Press and Publishing Development Company
F 7 Donghu Road, Shanghai, China (200031)
Email: comments_betterlinkpress@hotmail.com

Computer typeset by Yuan Yinchang Design Studio, Shanghai
Printed in China by Shanghai Donnelley Printing Co. Ltd.

1    2    3    4    5    6    7    8    9    10

# Contents

CONTENTS

# The Heartbeat of a City

## – Preface to the English Edition of
### *Voices from the Sea*

This anthology is a collection of verse written in recent years by poets who live and work in Shanghai.

Some might suggest that an ultra-modern city like Shanghai is an unlikely place to produce poetry. I beg to differ. Many important poets have been Shanghai residents who created their best work while in the city. They include, but are not limited to, Xu Zhimo, Dai Wangshu, Li Jinfa, Ren Jun, Xin Di, Wen Jie and Lu Mang. During the first half of the 20th century, various schools of poetry grew up in Shanghai, fostering the development of modern poetry in China. This collection of work by contemporary poets in Shanghai is a testimony to this fact.

Shanghai is a young, open-minded and vibrant city, where the meeting of east and west has long intrigued the world. The miseries and uncertainties it has suffered, and the long tortuous road it has traveled over the last century serve as sources of inspiration. The works in this anthology therefore portray both the exterior and

interior landscapes of contemporary Shanghai. In the past three decades, thanks to many reforms in China, Shanghai has undergone a vast transformation, which has been carefully studied by its poets. Their work alternately voices surprise, confusion, lamentation and aspiration, as well as expectations for the future. Their lines delineate a diversity of scenes and people peculiar to Shanghai and paint a picture of a city that is brimming with life. Poetry is the singing of one's inner voice; it is the free flight of one's thoughts and emotions. The poems collected here thus provide a reflection of the zeitgeist, a monitor of the heartbeat of a city.

The translation of poetry is a complex and difficult undertaking. The rhyme and rhythm of the original writing may change, but the feelings and thoughts of the poets still shine through. It is hoped that this collection will offer readers a glimpse of the shape of modern Shanghai, and let them catch the pulse of this unique city.

Zhao Lihong

3 July 2007

# Winter Catches Up with A Birch Tree

Only yesterday I was scattering golden
    leaves in the autumn breeze;
Today a cold wave freezes my feet in soil
And dresses the earth in flurries of snowflakes
Pouring down from the long, dark stretch of sky.

All my twigs are snapping, falling.
All I can do is wait as I fall apart
As a vast, silent and ruthless winter
Encircles me with a howling wind.

I shut my eyes and plunge deeper into the earth,
When my snaking roots meet with the tendrils
Of another, pushing past and urging:
Open your eyes and take a look!

What is there to see? A shroud of winter clouds?
The leaning masts poking up from the iced-over river?
— Open your eyes and take a look!
I open my eyes and stare back:

Before me is a sapling
Whose eyes are filled with tears of joy.

# Knowing Each Other

We are part of this land,

The cause of all our fortunes and misfortunes;

The mountain ranges are our bones,

The rivers our veins.

The incense spiraling up from the ruins of temples
    and palaces,

The huddle of thatched huts, cow pens and pig sties

Each hold our hearts and weigh up our fate

While history weighs us down, slows our progress.

We met in the days of the wolves and jackals,

When your muted call

Reached me from across the mountains.

I have never allowed myself to think of my own suffering,

But yours break my strength.

# Echoes of a Sigh

I have never wanted to be a hero,

All I want is to love and to be loved;

I am not anyone's rival, I would rather give than take.

My reputation as a strong character,

Has arisen from a misunderstanding.

I am simply a part of the silent majority,

Humming a few songs that spring to mind.

Who knew that a small sigh

Could trigger such a storm of echoes!

But I am as powerless to stop it

As to stop the singing of a mountain bird;

Nothing is more painful

Than having to tear out one's voice with one's own hands.

# Dialogue with Light

This is no metaphysics—

Sound without a body,
Light without a body—

These are amorphous things.

I slip between them,
Between form and formlessness.

I do not fear death —
Life will not survive
A billion years.
Therefore all I ask is this:
Will my soul — the root of poetry —

Will become like the light
Of lightning, the shock of electricity?

Only light can share this secret with the earth:
Surviving endless solitude.

# Steam Whistle

Silence does not suit you
Until the flame has flickered out.

Ring out—
You are the sky's shrill chime,
You are the windpipes of the ocean!
If children no longer shouted and whooped,
If man's voice stopped short,
If the seas fell silent,
If the world became mute,
Then it would be as if the throat
Of the entire universe had been pulled out.

# Vows

Words chiseled in stone
May yet get blown away,
Works set in ink
May still blur and fade.

A fleeting wisp of cloud
Will survive somewhere,
A falling meteorite
May disintegrate but is still there.

A hint of an unplanned smile,
A look from the depths of the heart,
Even the distant shudder of lightning,
Are far superior to thunderous,
    pompous vows of love,
Deep as the ocean, lofty as mountains.

# Streetlamp

Sometimes
I become a streetlamp
Left suspended in the somewhere of night
Waiting for people to pass by.

The road below is long
And thick with mud.
My faint light
Paints the passers-by,
Guiding them home
In the thick glow of my loneliness
And I am for now fulfilled.

I am not noticed
As they come and go,
Navigating a world of footfalls,

And slowly receding backs.
Their shadows slip from me
As if to say
There is not light enough even for us.

If I become a streetlamp again
I will not regret it—
The litany of footsteps
    and the parades of fading backs
Would extend the roaming light
Of my far-flung thoughts and flights of fancy.

# Holly

When the snowflakes begin to swirl
I discover
Your deep, stubborn passion —
A shock of green amid the winter grays,
A spark of fire from the pallid earth,
A dream of spring in a desperate heart.

When flowers bud and bloom
I forget you, blinded
By the riot of colors,
Drunk on the scent
Of bow and blossom.

I no longer envy the flowers
That lure swarms of butterflies and bees,
Since not all life
Is sung by color alone.
I would shed these vanities
To become one of you,
To be a plain and ordinary
Sprig of holly.

# The Last Flight

A wounded hawk
Has finally broken free from the tether that tied it down
And has soared into the sky.

The rope tore off one of its legs
A drizzle of blood-red rain
That it sacrificed for freedom.

To make its last flight
It marshaled all its strength
And buckeld against the pain.

It circled and circled
Wheeled and wheeled,
Then disappeared.

The hills and rivers collected its feathers
And its flesh and blood,
The blue sky embraced its soul.

# Nanjing Road

This is Nanjing Road—walk carefully.
Do not tread on the heels of those ahead,
Avoid being trod on by those behind;
Keep your face well away from the next face
Lest you breathe in a stranger's breath.
Watch your step—don't talk.

This is Nanjing Road—cutting edge of commerce,
Street of streets, road of roads.
Trod by feet from all provinces of China
And all corners of the globe,
A place of hesitant verbs
And carefully chosen words.

This is Nanjing Road—walk carefully.

Neons quiver and desires ebb and flow.
How far can this feast stretch
While wallets of all sizes bulge and tear.

This is Nanjing Road—faces shift
And become unrecognizable; clothes and jewelry
Telling people who you are.
Everyone here is away from home.

This is Nanjing Road—is it night
Or is it day? The eyes are in Paris
The ears in New York. Only the heart
Has no address. In the streams of people
There has to be a philosopher—
May I ask: where does this road lead?

# The Voice of Stone

Even in times when ordering a stone to speak its mind
Was considered normal,
The stones kept silent.

It was not that they were mute
Nor that they had nothing to say,
For stones have their own style and character.

Yet the writings etched in stones,
Or the shapes and forms carved from it,
Are distortions of the stone—

You may be able to smash a stone
But you cannot put words
In its mouth.

Stones speak only to the silent;
When I brought a stone home from afar
I heard it say "Glad to meet you…"

When I was about to throw it out one day,
I heard it say
"If only I had known…"

# Don't

Don't extinguish another's lamp
Just to make your own lamp appear brighter.

Don't block another's path
For there are thousands of ways to advance.

Don't believe you are the only one sober
    in a world of drunkards
For distinctions are not always so clear cut.

Don't think you are separate from the crowd,
Since all were born and all must die.

Don't give your life to a single idea,
When millions of different flowers might grow.

Don't be too smug, or you will risk sounding
Like a frog down in a well croaking out its
    opinions of the sky.

# The Human Heart

The human heart
Can be a sea
Of billowing waves.

It can be a lake
Reflecting the lazy clouds sweeping across the sky,
Undisturbed by wind or waves,
Gentle ripples spilling out in circles.

The human heart
Can be a swamp,
With sour stinking water, with murky depths
Of algae, jealousy and greed.

The human heart
Can be dry and lifeless well,
Which can only hold
A square meter of the sky's calm light.

# A Voice from Home

There is a certain sound
That evokes birds in flight,
Or schools of fish swimming in the ocean;
That resembles anticipation in a trek through a desert,
And the dreamy mistiness of spring rain.
It is a sound of dignity, solidity and sincerity
A sound of intimacy and tenderness.
This is the haunting voice
From my home country.

Messenger from home,
Balm to a tired traveler
When the long nights are exhausted by solitary musings,
And the tip of a cigarette flickers in the window.
When the flower of memory begins to wilt,
And the past begins to fade away

Only my native accent stays intact,
As fresh as the soil and the air of home.

A voice from home is as sweet as water
From a mountain spring in summer,
As fragrant as rain-washed jujube blossoms,
As bitter as a new tea of mid-spring vintage.
It is the light knocking on a door in a deserted alley,
The pitter-patter of autumn rain dripping from the eaves,
The whistle of pigeons gliding through the blue sky.
It is the winter fire in the inn for mule drivers,
The familiar sound of heavy snoring.

That accent from the slopes of my home
Is the main theme among a diversity of tongues,
The fortissimo note in the symphony of life.

It is the babbling, chattering brook that winds
    through the village;
Whether you stay in a luxury hotel
Or in a remote town, you can hear
The stream echoing the call of your heart.
It is the stars glittering in a clear night sky;
Whether you are trekking through a vast wasteland
Or navigating tortuous mountain trails, home
Is never far from your thoughts.
It is the morning fog enveloping the orange grove,
The pet name called out by a mother seeing
    off her child at the village bridge,
The folk tune hummed by the weaving loom
    under a scholar tree,
A wife's whispers among the silkworms,
The snapping wood clappers of a wandering
    peddler at night

The sound of washings being beaten at the village stream
    in evening twilight,
The trumpet call that summons the locals to an
    emergency repair of the dikes,
The noisy celebration of a bumper crop on the threshing
    ground,
The undercurrents that wash over the heart
And the first thumping thunderclaps of spring.
Whether you have roamed to the far corners of the world,
Or find yourself abroad in exile or errand
The voice from home will always call you back
Across the years.

# Traveler

Fog-like drizzle brushing against my cheeks
I set off from the small store, wine still on my lips.
The red beans of the south country are
    small tokens of love,
Now lost among a stomach full of memories and regrets;
Last night's bonfires are now ash and dirt.
To the sound of hoofs moving through the woods,
I follow a stream and skirt a hollow in the hills,
The range of mountain peaks in the rain
Reflecting a thread of blue clouds beaking loose.
Rocks drip with cascades of tears.
The forests and the birds best understand the traveler:

They perform a dance of falling leaves
And dedicate birdsong to him.
I drift with the clouds,
Destined to travel all my life,
Without a home to rest my tired head.
The stream laughs at me, this traveler from the south
Without a cantering horse or a wind-driven sail.
Little stream, bubbling with warmth
Why not accompany me?
Our common destination is the ocean
And the road ahead is long.

# Wild Spirits

Trailing a storm of howling sand
Wild horses sprint across the Gobi plains.

They do not know belonging,
Only the stretch of open spaces;
They have never been tamed
Or turned from the wilds of their nature.
They are born with tempers
In flame, wild spirits unloosed.

The sight of wild horses
Lets dreams slip their shackles.

# Song from South of the Yangtze

Sprouting in the bamboo grove,
Falling with the apricot blossoms,
And bobbing down the lazy brook,
Come this catalogue of memories.

My mother's smile to
The sound of Pa's pole pushing out the boat;
A cloud of peach blossom
And a wave of willows;
A gaggle of ducks
Before the silhouette of a sail;
A wisp of smoke spiraling up from a stove.
The bitterest of salty tears,
And the sweetest of dreams.

They sprout from the bamboo grove,
Fall with the apricot blossoms,
And settle gently in a misty drizzle
In a misty drizzle....

# Musings at Cape Lujiazui

All at once the sky has shrunk.
The clouds are daubed on
In the sharp hues slinking up from the highrises.
Concrete mixers and welding guns crunch and sing
In jutting buildings
Pushing up through the Shanghai sky.

The eagles of finance
Have flapped their giant wings here from the
    five continents,
Hatching grand plans.

Jittery melodies spill from the musical water show
At the public fountain:
Something about the future,
Something about hope.

# Freed

Fed on a certain mood
My days
Have grown long and hungry.

The strings of the hours have given up
On music and knotted
Into an impossible cocoon.

Or else they have tangled into a teardrop
That belongs to a girl harvesting mulberry leaves,
Who must be wondering where it has got to.

In the wait between one moment
And the next, sudden thunderclaps
Roll across a soundless landscape.

The knot is freed at last,
And your welcome hands
Have carefully restored it to silk.

# Recherche du Temps Perdu

Could it be that all that is gone
Is mourned by someone?
Mourning is not a rending but a steeping,
A splash of scattered scarlet petals
Floating in water.

Fond memories are hard to forget
And even painful experiences
Might acquire a sweetness in hindsight.
The balmy spring breeze feeds the fields,
While the lashing of a rain storm
Serve to quench the earth's thirst.

That past is a butterfly fluttering through the mind,
With neither pride nor regret;
The heart is the home of dreams,
Which speak of neither possibilities nor the impossible;
Yet why will this stream of moments
Not stop flowing by?

# Papa and His Wheelbarrow

When I was little
Papa pushed a wheelbarrow.
He arched his back as he pushed it
Across a bridge with an arched back.
Sweat streamed down between his shoulder,
A slim river that trickled through the rut trailing the cart
And leaked into a crack in my memory.

Since then the bridge has stood
Many storms and many summers,
Though the wheelbarrow has disappeared.
Only the squeaking of the wheelbarrow remains;
An unforgettable song
That springs from the loamy earth of home.

# Home

When Mom was alive
I missed her —
Home was
Where smoke rose up from her stove.

Now that Mom is gone
I miss her even more —
Back home
In peace she rests.

When it rains in my village, tears rain
Down on the hearts of the homesick.

# Balmy Breeze

I cannot translate May for you —
The balmy breeze of May
Cannot be captured by the work of words.

The world begins to buckle and curve:
The ripples on a lake,
Willow twigs in the wind,
Scenic routes slinking somewhere south of the Yangtze.

The morning glories that crept up the trellis,
Heads hung down in the rain,
Now scatter in the wind — they drift
On the wings of the wind,
A crowd on unfurling flying umbrellas
Each a patch of clarity,
A splash of sunshine, a bright skyful of color.

The beachcombing kids searching for treasure
Have become young lovers, their trawling spoons
Swirling coffee cups full of distant futures,
Seaside evenings and nights together,
Their hearts ground down to gold dust,
Like the coffee beans carried from afar.

Slip into your swimsuit,
Rest your head against the sand —
This pillow of the May breeze.
Do not let it slip through your fingers —
Once it is gone, all that will be left
Is a summer sweat, the endless
Nagging of cicadas.

# A Feeling

45

In the book of wind

Is a chapter of stillness,

And from one fluttering page

A breeze tears out a single letter

And scatters it: a handful of hyacinths.


I throw on an autumn coat:

A carefree soul

In a carefree breeze,

Unaware of the late rush of warmth

Or the bubbling red sunset breaking.


I pass window after window

With the wind as my messenger

Carrying my greetings.

No one knows
The hyacinth
Is a word waiting to be spoken.

As the world shakes,
The wind holds it still —
Usher of autumn and my autumn coat
And the long walks past strangers' windows;
Believe it or not, the wind
Has coaxed the hyacinths  into bloom.

# Beggar Girl

47

A cascade of pale golden hair
Like the silk of ears of corn,
Falling over a face bent down in prayer.

A childish frame bowing in the breeze;
The sun kneels before you
Like a tree that kneels before its fallen leaves.

# Leaving

Was our life together really a union of two souls?
Your breath wilted the leaves around me,
And seared and singed our hearts.
The world came crashing down: all our seasons
Set in this one season,
All our hopes handed over to loss.

The north wind turning up the night snow
Is wiping the path clear of yesterday's footsteps.
Though you sleep, your voice still fills the dark —
I am leaving, bequeathing only ashes
And a dead moon,
Buried in the depths of your eyes.

Sitting on the floor of a crowded southbound train
I leave behind the last spring, the buds withered
   on the vine.
I leave my old life behind, my dreams and songs,
Words and cries drowned out
By the roar of the locomotive engine.

# On Love

Love is an ancient question
Like a deep, ancient well.

I stare down the stone depths,
To the still water, the echoing voice;

The well tells me it has drawn deep
From the thirst of humanity that never dies.

I weave its words into a long rope
And begin a search for a bucket to draw water.

# In an Alley

A narrow streetscape:

I run through many years of rain and wind,

Through a tapestry of silk and satin

That has weaved itself into a winding alley,

Rutted and creased, crisscrossed by thick tangles

Of celebration and cobblestones loaded with sorrows.

Perhaps the sun, the moon, the stars

Have picked out my prayers;

Maybe my dreams and expectations

Have frozen in frustration

Or have been burned up in experience. I keep running.

Months and years drip from the eaves,

The roses glance out from windowsills

And smile; there is no such thing

As success or failure,

Youth or old age;

There is nothing but the alley

Stretching under my feet as I run.

# Ode to Nanpu Bridge

The Huangpu River says

"This belt is the borders of my dream."

The wind says

"What an amazing harp! Let me draw a celestial

tune from it."

The cloud says

"This is a swooping bar for metaphysical acrobatics."

The rainbow says

"My shadow has been welded to the river."

The bird says

"Ten thousand of us might settle here and still

have room to spare."

The engineer says

"The magic is in the blueprint."

The worker says

"This buckle has been forged from rivers of sweat."

The Shanghai local says

"The two banks of the river finally meet in the air!"

# Mama, Did You Hear?

Three years running I have cried out in my dreams —
Mama, did you hear?
This is the secret language of the earth,
Words that keep the heart warm.

My call to Mama
Remembers her labor in my birth,
The months and years of struggle and support,
The way she pointed out the path
Down which my thoughts flow.

I cry out again and again —
Mama, can you hear me?
Thousands of miles apart,
The wind will carry your reply.

# Red Bean Cafe

Surrounded by success, I take a swig
   from the cup of failure,
— A failsafe recipe has failed to work,
An anticipated arrival did not appear —
How bitter this brew has become!
On the first day we met, everything I thought I might say
Shriveled to a stuttered question or two.
I fell asleep with your name on my tongue
And sunlight punctured my dreams,
You showed up unexpected, and now that I expect you,
You have gone.
You are an assassin of the minutes, of the hours,
   of the days.

Yet in all strength lurks tenderness, in all answers
Are other hidden questions.
Was it fear or was it something else,
That let you leave? I cannot know;
No two hearts are the same.
Mine sinks into dribbles of swirling coffee,
Thinking back of that winter night that I should
    not have walked into.
I might drink your bitter shadow, drain
    the dregs of memory,
But still this bitter hunger.

# Before a Bronze Statue of Pushkin

Your head held high as defiant as ever,
Scanning the far horizon, letting the wind snag
The last of your wandering thoughts.
Your bronze bust is no gold-leaved Buddha
Yet your words curl out like cloistered chants,
Stinging the other statues into action.
Your sharp sword glistens with a cold resolve
And cuts my slurred dream to the quick.

# In Vino Veritas

57

This glass of wine steeps time
And shades the light with sorrow and elation.
The bubbles brim with conversations,
Clinking glasses, swirling the wine,
People mingle with stinging tongues —
In the depths of the brimming glass
I find my own reflection.

# Writing by Candlelight

After a sudden power cut
All the faces faded into darkness
And all the verses dimmed

Until the breath of a candle
Brought us back to ourselves
In the shimmer of its shining wick.

It threw our silhouettes
Across the wall
And dragged them into our verses.
The candle shed its thick, glistening tear;
We are all candles shedding tears,
Burning tears as kindling for our poems.

# Under the Lamp

The calm night is dimpled by the din of firecrackers
Ushering out the old year.

The midnight lamp flickers
On my wife, sewing a dress for our daughter.
The trailing thread is pulled ahead by her needle
Tugging up a sparking sunrise.

The new year creeps in the door
And our daughter teases out the spring,
Takes the seasons in hand.

# Nameless River

You saunter so contentedly
Between fields of buckwheat and cotton,
Hordes of wild flowers and white poplars
Crowding at you sloping banks.

You have none of the whitewater rapids of the Yangtze
Or the tempestuous waves of the Yellow River;
Yours is a slow waltz fleeting through the landscape
To the accompaniment of a whistling willow.
You feed the plains, the scudding clouds
And the murmurs of spring swallows.

I envy you, nameless river,
Winding toward the horizon
Leaving your feelings lapping at the banks.

When my life seems small
I search out the distance
For the ripples in your shimmering skin,
Slipping away.

# Water of Jiang'nan

{Jiang'nan: areas south of the Yangtze River}

The vast stretch of Jiang'nan
Resembles a splayed out mulberry leaf.
Its rivers, densely woven warp and woof,
Recall the veins of the leaf;
To try to leave is always a tangled affair,
A skein of strings and threads impossible to unravel.

Jiang'nan is made of water:
Gray-tiled houses overlooking the water,
   slate-paved roads beside it,
A mass of hands muddling through the shallows
And the soles of shoes sloshing through puddles
   and streams.
Women wash their laundry in their reflections:
It clears for their peering faces, gives them grace.

Locals living by the river
Get to moor their dreams on the water's edge;
Those further away

Might dig a well in the yard
To bring the deep murmurs of river tides to their homes,
And let watery mists envelope their garden.

Jiang'nan people wrap themselves in water
And call it silk,
Then slip through streets as fish through water.
They might wander into a teahouse
And drop a pinch of *biluochun* tea leaves into
    a boccaro teapot
As if steeping their happiness in the secrecy of their heart.

Once someone attempted suicide by jumping into
    the water:
Yet almost as soon as he took the plunge
He clambered back to the shore —
It is said when a person comes in contact with water
All his melancholy is washed away.

# Old Tree

Alone on the seashore
Like an old man at sunset —
The hoar of long years creeping across your temples,
Wrinkles slinking over your bare torso —
Only memory keeps you going.

You have finished your slow growth
You bows to spring sunshine
Your push to the sky.

Your existence was a secret kept by the land,
Fed up through soil to branches and leaves.

You are a silent guard, keeping watch
Over noiseless fields and plains.

Often in dreams
I stumble across your silhouette against the sky,
And hear the music of your scattered twigs:
The falling leaves, I imagine
Are the greeting cards sent by autumn to spring.

# Passing a Museum

The museum is history's stage,

Where the spectators are pottery figurines

And an earthen pot gives accounts of past glories.

Our ancestors awake

To the accompaniment of feral musical notes,

village women rise amid flames,

Caught in airy, undulating lines, captured on canvas.

In those distant year our forebears

Twisted their earthworm waists in dance —

A thousand years of burning desire

Shaping the curves into firm thrusting breasts,

Bamboo slips and black butterflies' enigmatic acrobatics.

Next, a Song Dynasty village

Filled with the mysteries of symbols

Like a celestial lamp

Unable to fathom the secrets of the world.

A procession of Tang walls and Song bricks,

Ming porcelain and Qing jade

And cobwebbed eaves with knife-like teeth.

There is a black butterfly in flight,

Its wings breaking as it flutters through windows:

Wisdom flickers and dims

And the trail leading to the future loses its way.


A thousand years of civilization

Has been reduced to a storm in an earthen pot.

The first to emerge is a village woman following

A trail lit by the fresh-discovered fire;

It extends into the distance

Beyond which the eye cannot see.

# Quiet Beauty

Dawn comes treading quietly under the trilling of birds;
Teardrops limber to the tips of blades of grass and
    outstretched branches.
The soft spring breeze wrinkles the face of the dark lake
And rustles the gossamer skirts of young girls;
A pastel sunset is washed over by a wave of night.
Daylight is a moistened yellow handkerchief
And the snow is the colour of moonlight
On the sandy beach.

Smoke curls up from a peasant's kitchen
Like the memories blooming from an old man's long-
    stemmed pipe;
The *longjing* tea on an office desk is cold and weak
And idle thoughts are sipped and swallowed.

Neighbors in the same alley keep a distance from
    door to door
For these are the careful terms of dispassionate  love.


A history that never changes is bland, useless,
Like antique vases with sleepy eyes.
A spell has been cast on the nation —
Occult melodies ebb and flow through our blood
Yet our desires hide themselves
Beneath a bland character, beneath convictions
And beliefs and hoary, tangled ethics.
Generation after generation
We plod on
Into gentle oblivion.

# A Tanker Truck

Every day at the same time
And in the same place
The tanker truck crawls along a winding road;
Forehead against my car window I gaze
At the numerals on its side, their colors fading
As it slithers like a maggot on a winding path
Every day at the same time
And in the same place.

Every day at the same time in the same place at
   the same speed
The tanker truck comes collecting resentment
With its grimy numbers on its grimy side.

I've lost the nerve to gaze out my window
My own car crawling like a maggot behind it.

Maybe I should go to sleep,
But maybe I can't fall asleep.

# Pottery

Pottery: history battered in by darkness
And forged in fire.
An accidental bonfire
Blazing for nine thousand years.

Potsherds with cord patterns found at Immortals' Cave
Put an end to a barbaric epoch;
The dancers on the painted Majia Kiln earthenware
Interpreted the earliest dreams of our ancestors.

Pottery is a prologue to more civilized times,
With wavy lines of unbroken chains of mountains
And meandering rivers, star-studded skies.
Strange patterns and winding designs
Depict the bravery of hunting
And the toils of farming
While grotesque totems
Murmur of the deeper mysteries of being alive.

Pottery is the closest companion of humanity,
A witness of the departure of the rains and winds
Of a thousand autumns,
While keeping its own color safe from flight.

Yet in this time of lust and greed
Where is the pottery we need
To slash and burn to break new ground
In the wilds of the human heart?
For pottery still calls for an end of barbarism
For a return to light.

# Clock Hands

In childhood, the two clock hands
Resemble a pair of chopsticks
With which to pluck up morsels
To feed a rumbling, hungry belly.

In the middle of life, the two clock hands
Resemble two long legs forever in a hurry,
Leaving behind them
A hundred grubby footsteps.

In old age, the two clock hands
Resemble a sharp pair of scissors
Cutting time into flakes of snow
To cover one's crown and temples.

One of these days
The two clock hands will turn
Into the twin poles of a stretcher
Which lifts you to a far and lofty heaven.

# A Pond of Withering Water Lilies

Not long ago
You were flittering your large, twinkling eyes
As your lily pads danced in the breeze.
No sooner had a falling leaf heralded the onset of autumn
Than you were dappled with wrinkles, age spots and
    blotches,
With sallow skin and thinning hair,
A gaunt face swollen ankles and limping legs.
Unkempt, untidy and undone
Your ornate looking glass
Has now been clouded over with algae.
On a moonless night
The switchblade autumn wind gives chase
As some leaves lie supine,
Some stoop or droop,

Bend at the waist or kneel on one leg,

While still others weep or fall flat,

But not a drop of blood is in sight.


Shadows and ghosts

Float in your reflection;

Lotus-white hands will not

Brush winter from your face.


Note: Traveling with the poets Lu Hong and Qian Tao in Shezhong Villiage, Huzhou on 3 November, 2006, I was shaken by the sight of a pond full of withering water lilies, which inspired this poem.

# You

Everyone contains a 'you'
And every 'you' is distinct.

Some are like a pristine spring in the mountains;
Some the murk of a muddy pond.

Some are the turquoise waves of West Lake
Carrying the fragrance and grace of miles of water lilies;

Some are like Suzhou Creek
With dark swirling ripples;

Some are sun-filled rainbows of many colors
Or golden sunflowers,

Some the gloom of autumn raindrops
And dark forest lichen.

Maybe you are a pine tree high up in the hills,
Watching the day creep from dawn to dusk,

Or perhaps you are a weeping willow by the water,
Contemplating your rippling mirror image.

Some 'you's twitter on slim branches,
While some soar and into the vastness expanse of sky;

Some 'you's are a winter in the heart of spring,
Some the greenness of spring striking through winter.

'You' has a million faces, a billion hearts
Each with its hundred plans.

# Two Lines of
# Verse That Will Not Let Go

Two lines of verse that will not let go

Are lodged among lofty peaks;

They undulate with the bumps of the winding road,

Hold tight to the rushing roar of the river

As it drives across the highlands.

As the rhythm quickens and quickens,

Chasing a bank of clouds like a giant dragon

The lines spill from the page, and give us hope.

We read and reread and these two lines cling on,

When all else is gone, for poetry is nothing

If not for aspiration and desire.

# Ice

My pain is a sliver of ice, a dart
Frozen behind my eyes,
The dark ink that draws the world away.

My friend, come no closer —
In the warmth of your palm it might melt
Down to dribbles and streams —
And I cannot let that happen,
For in the heart of that shard of ice
Is my first innocence frozen tight.

# The Window of Time

The jagged rock of life
With its odds and ends and nuts and bolts
Can be cut by the craft of imagination
Into a shining diamond.

It takes the frustration of certainties made uncertain
To rub and scrub
The window of time to transparency.
Look through: the forking paths
Call you back to where you stopped and turned
Or turned again; a hundred other pasts you did not find.

Staring between the potholes and bumps in the path
I found myself, returning somewhere.

# That Leaf

You sent me a leave from a tree
In a distant country, carried here
By a friend. It is a bookmark now,
Pressed between the pages of a favorite book.

Does that stranger of a tree blossom?
With the leaf's fluttery arrival
My favorite book
Has spread and bloomed
With budding thoughts of you.

# Winter Day

In the first morning light of the last stretch of the year
A single star glistens
In the paling sky.

Light from a great distance,
Its dimmed brilliance
Shines through the fog of my breath.

Is this me —
This jumble of feeling, this mess of hopes?
I have searched a thousand places for it.

Perhaps it is too late — soon the night
Will evaporate into memory
Like the hair falling from my forehead,
Showing something of the way
I see myself.

The winter sun is now high in the sky

# A Complaint

83

Amber complains deep in the ground:
My beauty is in vain.

Coal complains deep down in the ground:
My burning passion is wasted.

Only the seeds do not complain
But resolutely push out from beneath the soil

To grow into lofty red pines
Or graceful dragon spruces.

# White Conch

Those supposed to listen,
Listen day and night

To the rise and fall of crests and troughs,
To the soft swaying of the mast tops and the
    quivering of feathers

And weave from them a song of the sea.
Time washes over the past, over worries and regrets,

Together with footprints and words,
All cleansed by the crashing waves.

All that is left is a vast flat of sand,
Rows of palm trees, a flaxen shoreline,

And a serene star-studded sky;
Stars and gladioli above spiky cacti.

The invisible pull of the sun and the moon,
And the fermenting tides of swirling sea salt,

Have given your grains a sparking shine
The white of the waves, the gulls and the clouds.

Those supposed to listen, listen eternally,
Made humble by the constant molding.

I approached your wavelike radial ribs
And brought back a resonant ear.

# Writing

I roll sky and earth into a pen,
And slice time into sheaves of paper;
With the material of strange lives
I craft lines of characters,
The stuff of endless writing.

# Purple Starfish

Even the mighty sea is powerless to save its own;
The disappearance of a life is no longer news.
In the vast spray of seething waves,
In small baskets on a small beach
I thumb through starfish tagged for sale.

Queen starfish, princesses of milk-white
Coral forests  and moon-gray jellyfish,
Specked with purple and settled
Among the horseshoe and tiger-striped shells.
I pick one up and pay, a lone planet
In the hollow of my palm,
Stiffened to compass points.

The five feelers still sharp
And self-confident, but also melancholy,
   whispering
That you miss the ocean —
The schools blowing blue translucent bubbles
And the games of hide-and-seek
From which the baby sharks were banned.

Perhaps in the shattered hulks of sunken ships,
Between rusted anchors and broken masts,
In silk handkerchiefs showing blossoming lotus
That settled on the ocean floor
You had a glimpse of human secrets,
Though the humans behind them remain hidden.

Perhaps you wonder how far you have come
From that winding coral forest;
I begin to regret
Using your frozen tears
To adorn a speechless wall
And pierce a corner of my heart.

Not all good acts
Receive the respect they deserve,
Nor is all hurt planned.
Starfish, let's be friends —
My heart will be your coral forest.
In my eyes and the eyes of those around you,
You rise to the top of the mountains in the distance.

# Beautiful Rain

Flicking your long sleeve,

You enveloped me and told me to follow you

So I followed,

Staggering and light-headed.

At a crossroads

You stirred the air with a handful of flying twigs

And torn-up mushrooms began to soar through the street.

In road of lost faces with drink-misted eyes

And lost dreams, you told me to get close

To every one of them,

And I did.

Leaning against a sopping billboard

I suddenly felt an urge to cry out:

"Listen, you city dwellers —

Your houses are far too cramped,

Your buses too crowded,

Your prices too high,

And you try to be too perfect!"

Why is it that only at these times,

Caught in the midst of a downpour,

Do we acknowledge each other and smile?

At all other times

Of sunlight and wind,

We become strangers

Wearing poker-faces through the streets.

# Musings in a Street from the Past

The streetlamp shone dimly
On a narrow old street of low houses;
A gust of autumn wind swept the cobble-stoned street,
Polishing the speckled stones to a new smoothness.
The night of rain had left the air crisp and cool,
Though everyone had succumbed to the warmth
    of hearth and home;
I stood alone at the side of the deserted street,
Letting a river of reflections spill out from me.

Footsteps pounded down the street of my childhood —
The rhythms of the past approached at a leisurely tempo
And a girl breezed by, a bloom ready to burst
    from the bud;
She turned to look at me and then was gone.

I stalked her shadow, followed the echo of her heels,
Down the street and across an old bridge.
Beside the bridge a two-storied house,
A strange mixture of Chinese and Western styles,
Exuded the fragrance of books —
From its lamp-lit window
Floated the soft strains of the "Red Raspberry Blooming",
Making me think of Tonia Tumanova.

I stood in the deserted street
Trying to retrace a past now lost
In the relentless spinning of minutes and hours.
In the distance someone was knocking on a door,
And night spread out softly
Like a woman's black skirt in a breeze.

# Music

The cool light of the moon casts a misty shroud
Over the green and the concert hall sitting in its center;
The yellow glow sweeps over the long oval,
And I find myself at the beating heart of this serenity.

I imagine the flow of a pulsing river of music
     inside the hall,
Beethoven's roaring, untamed Eroica
Or the dreamy murmurs issuing forth from
     Mozart's strings.

Turning around I was brought back
To a world of car lights roaming like sinuous
    swarms of fireflies,
A jagged skyline of high-rises
And the countless blinking eyes scoring
    through the night sky.

I raise my arms,
My blood pulsing and surging,
And slip into the vibrant song of life.

# You Make the Sky and the Earth Recede

From the fog of my consciousness
I hope to dedicate all that I have written
And all that I shall write
To you.

Draped in a cloak woven from the wind of the
    Yellow River,
You sailed into my sight
And whipped up the waves in the sea of my heart.

Even slumped quietly in a chair
You evoked whitewater rapids —
Pulling me swiftly
Into your driving currents.

The sky and the earth receded for you.
The world spun furiously to keep pace
And my eyes became lost in your ellipsis of a smile.

I would trade ten dark nights of melancholy
For one morning with you.
You searched my innocence for footnotes,
Not knowing that poetry has none.

# China's Address: 1983

Emerging from a long corridor
In the Museum of History
I ran smack into the seven-o'clock sun.
Workers in front of the newly finished milk-white
   apartment building
Are nailing in the address plaque:
Number 1983 in a street named The Future.

I catch sight of the wreckage of Epang Palace,
And the ruins of the Old Summer Palace,
And the fading gilt inscriptions hung above their gates,
The soaring calligraphy looping away from a lost epoch.

All around me
The roads of China are pulsating,
Flowing with sunlight

And flooded by early morning editions of newspapers,
Which talk of statues in town squares,
Crumbling old buildings and new jutting balconies.

The streets shift with the thousands
Of new buildings, a sea of blue door plaques;
No more rooftops crowded like swallow hatchlings,
Sheltering the secrets of three generations living together.
The sun rises each day on a different street,
Beaming through every window of every home
And spilling over the bright sky.

Beyond the fluttering ribbons waiting to be cut,
I spot girls from architectural colleges

Handing out certificates of occupancy to a smiling crowd;
Every shining key
Opens up a new prospect,
Lays a foundation of hope and possibility.

The metallic glint
Of the door plaque of China
Shines on the three thousand years of history behind me;
Between dreams and reality
A row of numerals stand tall:
1983 —
Gateway to the future.

# Sheep and Man

Sheep are lucky animals,
Weak-willed and always lumbering after others,
They place themselves at the mercy of the world.
Man eats sheep, and in turn
Man is devoured by other beasts.

You cannot fight your nature;
It can take lifetimes to grasp this simple truth.

In my village
Sheep are kept solely for their meat
Their lives are a wait in a pen
For the day of slaughter.

I have grown up with the sheep outside their pens —
I am also weak-willed and long for company,
Placing myself at the mercy of others.
I know myself only too well
And find myself crying out:

'Sheep! Don't you ever think
About what is happening to you?'

Sheep on the grassland,
So many tufts of unruly cloud.
Their character precedes them;
Only the vast grassland can accommodate them,
Can provide shelter for their vibrant, bleating lives.

At the sight of the a horde of sheep approaching
You cannot help but be overwhelmed
By a premonition of being swallowed up,
And be struck by the realization
That man is also so weak-willed.

# The Bund

Cloistered in this city

I often pass you by in a hurry.

One morning

I listened with my face turned skyward

To the tolling of the bells of the river-soaked Custom
    House

And my thoughts drifted back to the winds of the 19th
    century,

That must have raged cold and ruthless

Sweeping away the muddy flats and sandy shoals

While the Gothic and Greek architecture,

The granite and spires

Began to grow

Along the shore of this little fishing village.


Some are drawn to the scenery of Lijiang

Or the old walls of Beijing; yet these clusters

Of buildings draw tourists from faraway lands

Come to study these bronze rings on doors
And these round sculpted pillars.

The cold and silent marble,
With its long months and years dusted off,
Remains intact
While blue-eyed bankers
Stride across the waterfront.
Placing my hand on the wall and caressing its surface
I felt a bone-chilling coldness.
I could only stare in silence,
Willing my eyes to find some sparkle
In the lights of high finance reflecting off the rippling
    river,
And dancing over the city.
I stood against the railings
And saw the buildings slowly emerging from the river.

# Alley of Imagination

Perceptions and values bristle like teeth on a comb,
While certainty belongs to the past,
Transformed by mass production.
I let my imagination loose on the rooftops
Set densely in the alley like scales on a fish.

Someone takes out a bamboo armchair.
Turning a corner one finds shade from the summer heat;
Between dark tiles and whitewashed walls
I catch sight of a girl from an ordinary family,
Setting off a train of musings: Will my thoughts
End in poverty, bad times and ruin?
In the end I turn from the alley
In case the unfamiliar scene
Should slip into my dreams —
I stand gazing a long while at the entrance of the alley,
Though I am only passing by.

# Little Wooden House

In the heart of the city,

Clusters of tall buildings dressed in billboards

Nudge and push against each other as they rise,

Riding into the tide of clouds.

Only this small wooden house remains,

Squat and serene in the shadow of the high-rises.

The fine grain of the wood

Evokes the long breath of a forest,

The warmth of a fire in winter.

Filled with ancient folk tales,

It endures,

Silent but persistent —

If a wooden house were built to hold the soul,

Tell me, would it be lonely or serene?

# White Magnolia

Through the wet night it shone
The entire night through;
It stayed in my sight
Even while the wind was delivered by the drizzle.
A shimmering light
In the depth of the dark,
In a night of rain and wind;
A flower without leaves
In a dream of lies,
I acknowledged its silent truth.

# I Tore up a Poem I Wrote Yesterday

Yesterday I tore up a poem I wrote.

There was a girl
    Standing in the muddy rain,
Ice-cold raindrops from her umbrella
    Wetted the tips of her hair.
The rain
    Clung to the sleeves of the wind
And a stray kite spiralled
    Away from the waving arms of a child.
The glint in her eyes was taken away in the beak
Of that neighborhood bird who should have known better.

I tore up a poem I wrote yesterday.

At noon the sun
Was splayed across the sky,

And the narrow shadow of the girl
    Was tugged loose by the roaring wind;
Shreds of paper swirled
    Like flakes of fine snow.
She picked up the flashcards on the balcony
    That she uses to teach children to read,
And the memories hung out to dry
    Were folded and placed in a corner of the suitcase.
When evening crept in
    She put a stamp on an envelope of clouds
And a song without sound
    Settled in her heart.


Tomorrow, I feel sure, every word I write
Will flourish into a glowing bud.

# A Garden

The garden is a lazy humpback whale
Shuffling through an afternoon.
That geyser severed from its source
Sprang from the whaler's daydream.

The garden moves beyond him,
Its deep music calling up wild mushrooms
Hallucinogenic toadstools, flowers curling
Into letters and words in the book of an afternoon
That cannot help but shift its shape.
A reader enters the illustrations
And is transported to the land of legends

To be the whale's helpless wife
Caught in the web of endless imagination.

Poetry is a place where anything can happen,
Where worlds spring up from knots in words,
Where writing wells from a garden of desire.
That garden is a lazy humpback whale
Shuffling through a poet's passion.
That music of the geyser singing to the air
Has a source near extinction.

# Messenger God

The pair of green wings on the helmet of
    the messenger god,
At the top of the post office, are dedicated to flight.
The building has been nicknamed the edifice of light.
Under the morning stars, as day dawns and
    keeps dawning
The silhouette of the post office is a sound made solid,
A sound of bells tolling through the half-dark.
The profile of the post office is one part
Of the poetry of the north bank of the Suzhou Creek.
The bell tower sitting on its shoulders
Is a green reflection of the ooze beneath the bridge below.

Its shadowy gloom lurks in its west,
Where it will not fade into the night.

A sweeper shuffles his broom as
A milkman steals a glance at the plump buttocks
Of the daughter of the corner tobacconist.
Light inches into the dark, yet the light
Of the post office still hides
A more complete darkness.
The stone-gated *shikumen* and the old floodgate bridge.
As the high tide rises on the flats of the past,
A postman on a bicycle glides down a steep slope.

# Moon of Jiang'nan

Under the moon of Jiang'nan
The lights on the lake form a kaleidoscope of
   dancing color.
It paints a watercolor, in sharp lines
Of light and shade,
Depicting roofs with upturned eaves and tilted corners,
Over soaring whitewashed walls.

Under the moon of Jiang'nan,
Houses dot the landscape
Like stars in the sky or pieces on a chessboard.
The homes of Jiang'nan

Unfold from an endless scroll,
Dusted by misty moonlight
And written in the language of the heart.

Moonlight, lake lights,
Reflections of faces and low-hanging willows.
The waters of Jiang'nan glitter and sparkle
And never grow dim.

# Long Live Passion

Long live passion!

We have no need to ask the world for glory —
All we seek
In our short life spans
Is to let a gleam of light shine on across the universe
Through our children and students,
And to sculpt a lasting monument for the world
By growing a greater green forest on the globe.
This will be the meaning of our existence,
Our most lasting achievement,
And the only motive worth shedding tears for.

In the same way, we are thrilled
By the sight of people responding to a noble cause;
For when we truly succeed in making our hearts burn
In a shared passion, our resolve
Will swell into a storm that cannot be stopped
And bring comfort to all.

Life—we want to bring you warmth
Instead of sighs of humiliation and moans of weakness.

Awake the storm in your heart —
Let passion live forever!

# Pair of Boxing Gloves Hanging
# in a Busy Street

In this busy street, where each day crates of red
    wine are sold,
Hangs a pair of black leather boxing gloves
Offered for sale.

They are as genteel as a gentleman,
As quaint as a folk artist;
In a world of silk summer dresses
This pair of boxing gloves stand out.

No customer shows an interest
Yet
The muscles of a busy street begin to feel a secret pride.

A pair of boxing gloves
Have the appeal of a looming sports dome —
Like guests from Africa and South America
They only take part in international matches.

This pair of boxing gloves
Turned dark in sunlight
Have left their bruises on many skins.

Endowed with speed and a dynamic arc
They might reach a right hook up to the clear blue sky.

The pair of boxing gloves are a favorite classical tune;
Yet in China the modern tempo of the Black
   God is recognized
Rumbling down the busy street of life.

The pair of black boxing gloves
Fill the passers-by with fascination, and become
The city's treasured scenic route.

The hanging pair of black leather boxing gloves
Are an exotic legend or a glimpse of the future,
Compelling the fragrant wind to accept
The unstoppable nature of force.

# River

You are a pulsing liquid flowing
Through my veins toward the expanding,
Intensifying aspirations of my heartbeat;
Like a thawing dawn gilding morning-misted eyes
It unleashes echoes through the corners of my body.

You are so fluid, so quick,
As sinewy as the flexed-muscles of a masculine arm.
You fill the thirst of a blooming shrub in a coy romance.
You are that spring hidden deep inside winter,
You are the joy of the sunlit air, the bees' fast
    beating wings.
Your rapids, steeped in sequins of starlight,
Race with a boisterous roar.

Rivers are the oldest legends, their life prolonged by
    perpetual motion
And an ever churning whirl of emotion.

The noon sun plumbs the depth of the river
And a lone boat navigates an eddy,
Fast receding into the distance.
This is my life, flowing quietly
And recognized only from a distance:
Another insignificant retreat.

As the mist rises, riding over white sails negotiating
    strong currents,
I learn the language of the gulls,
Their murmured confidences amid the lapping froth.
The river is like a deep tune melting into the universe;
On its bank scalding drops slink from my forehead
To sink to the bottom of the river
Only to be swiftly swept away.
A fishing net is thrown into the water
In search of stories disappearing in the dark of night.

The story will go on, for the river
Still roars and forges ahead,
Like the stubborn trains steamrolling the
    rails on the riverbank
Or the trees and houses growing up beside it.

The river drives on its course
Toward a vast blue expanse — the ocean,
A more primitive power,
Drawing in rivers of relentless water;

From here on out, there are no more riverbanks.

At the estuary, I am awestruck by a dawning fact
Blood and water are the fluids of life.

# For a Long Time Now

For a long time now
I have prayed for peace.
Solitude no longer threatens to flood my thoughts,
Rather it is love itself
That marks a path between my thoughts.

For a long time now
A tree has shared its inner self
With me:

At night
I open my palms
And, like blades of grass
Receive rain and dew from the sky;

As dawn pushes up
I shiver with a rash of leaves;

For a long time now
I have contemplated
The flowers at my feet —

You must have noticed
The lines of concern
Written in wrinkles on my forehead.

# My City Becomes
# a Construction Site

From one day to another I find my city
Turned into a construction site —
A construction site of spring
Blistering with noise.

The air reverberates with the roar of machines.
This construction site of our city
Is ringing out a booming song
As it marches into the future.
It rises in a swirl of heroic colors,
The sun toasting its shining chest
And gilding its soaring thoughts.
There will be no more songs whispered
To empty rooms, only smiles drifting down
From the tallest of blocks.
I wield my pen to add to the work
Of conjuring up a city.

# Song without Words

We are enveloped by a hoarse voice
Just as the sleeve of grief is enveloped by a black
    mourning band.
Our tears have dried up;
Why is it that we may only live once?

Someone brushes by and I turn
And cheek to cheek we embrace
Giving vows to our hearts.
The May flowers disperse in the sudsy southerly wind
And break away from life.

We are enveloped by a hoarse voice
Which whispers to us to kill, to hate, to forget

In this age of venting and ranting
Are we capable of hearing anything at all?
We all have hands dripping with blood.
A clean break is the only option left.

Clear cold water flows through the cracks of our fingers
Then disappears.
We have nothing but this hoarse voice
To turn to now.
Our bodies become trees with white flowers, lawns of
 green grass
As we try and turn from our failures,
From the thousands of faults laid at our door.

# A June Afternoon

A June afternoon —
Full-bodied women wielding scythes harvest the wheat,
Laughing and chatting,
Wiping sweat from their brows with the front of
    their blouses.

Cottony white clouds coalesce around the sun;
Pillars of the earth lie across fields of dense grass
Interspersed with red and blue wild flowers
And gaggle of ducks swims slowly along one side
    of a river
Populated by their shifting reflections.

On a June afternoon
Sparrows attacked by women in the wheat fields
Scatter in fright,
But linger in the tree tops, waiting for their chance.

# Long Journey after Some Wine

The twilight looms like an illusion,

Like a long journey after some wine.

The storm lamp is lit, the sheet rain

Tightly hugs your lonely back

As I see you off on a long journey after some wine;

I watch the tails of your clothes

Whipped up by the wind.


The azure autumn sky

Tries to banish

The reeling rain

From the tin roofs of my home town.


You will not return

From the long journey after the wine

To show me your tattered youth;
Your innocence
Moves like a wild horse
Through the evening twilight,
Finally tugged free by the wind.

On a long journey after wine
A lone figure steps over ten thousand heads
And merges with the free-flowing fog.
Who is it that sits straight-backed in silence?
The evening twilight is an illusion
Stretching to the horizon
With a melancholy sigh.

# First Day of Autumn

Autumn sits in the cup of the early chrysanthemum,
Prayers brim over the riverbanks.
Our kisses spill out like lucid flames,
Wrapping themselves around our glistening skin.
The summer roses have left eye-catching corollas,
Which will stay to watch over autumn.
A dark green chrysanthemum
Is planted on the sea floor of this soul-stirring day.

I will be your true woman under the autumn moon.
In the theater of autumn you are the only player,
Shrouded in the thick curtains of light and shadows
Pouring out a lifetime of melodies that glitter like gems.
Let me hang beneath your breath
Let me be your most tender rib and arm,
In a dance with in the sun, the moon and autumn wind,
That finds its heartbeat in a breath.

# The Last Subway Train

The subway trains rumble through the bowels of the city,
Carrying meetings, greetings and goodbyes.

This is the day's last train.
The station platform is nearly deserted
As the carriages rattle in,
Bleary headlights scanning the night.

After seeing her off
I am unable to hum or whistle as others might;
Only by whispering her name
Do I feel a warmth permeate my body.

Sitting alone in the half-empty carriage
Staring past a crowd of unfamiliar faces
I think back to when we arrived,
While the roaring train
Carries me farther from the past.

The subway plays tricks,
Shortening the distance between us;
It soothes my panicking heart
Only to ruthlessly pull me away
Leaving me feeling like a stranger
In my own city.

When day breaks
The god of sleep comes knocking on my door.
The last train keeps juddering along
Zigzagging before my eyes.
I stand on a deserted platform
Watching her silhouette disappear,
Then reappear in the interstices of
        the rocking carriages —
How much longer, how long now?

# A Bar on Hengshan Road

People do not come here for the drinks
Since the wine list here
Features prices that will make
Even the most diehard drinker flinch.

Take my example.
I come here to be pulverized
By the deafening music
Before blowing home like a cloud of dust.

I come here to be surrounded by sultry beauties
Dressed in a torn patch of the night
And moving with a shudder of stars.

The faces swinging above the high heels
Resemble Pound's petals
On a wet, black bough.

Every petal is
A promise of spring.

No food to go with my drink;
Nursing a single beer
I linger there until closing time.

# Only the Sky Retains its Clarity

The moisture-laden clouds and mists maintain
    their silence
As I look down at my own reflection from high above.
A head full of thoughts is lightly shaken,
And a premonition of an impending storm shudders
    through my body.
I feel no lethargy, no wavering nor impatience;
I have no bouquet of tears fresh as the flowers in May.
I turn my back on everything graceful, and dream
Of dissolving slowly by the railing of a well

I imagine a ray of light penetrating my life,
A place shrouded in gloom and overcast by dark clouds;

If I listen closely I can hear deep underground murmurings
In a language of pale and unintelligible daylight.

Power is an intense flame scorching the earth,
obscuring the sun in burning colors,
blowing the dark clouds from their home.
Only the sky remains free.
Thunder shoots down its roaring roots,
Lightning dances on the wings of the bats;
Only the sky retains its clarity.

# Li Yu, The Last Emperor of Southern Tang

The last note
Of a tune
Plucked by your fingers
Is like the turn of fortune in the beak of a bird;
It is no fault of yours.

The wilted leaves
Will be harvested by the wind;
The pears have ripened
Though the cicadas have ceased their chanting;
You were a lousy Last Emperor,
But a master poet.

Under a crescent moon
Sloping over the eaves of the West Pavilion
With its fading red balustrades,

There is no possibility of sleep
Though the candle is spent and the hourglass stopped.
There is still a pot of wine,
A bamboo flute
And skein of romantic sentiments;
Reason enough to remember
The mountains and rivers of the old country.

# Rainy Night in the City

It rained all night in the city,
Pouring down drops of melancholy
In a low and deep chant, in a gilt bass
Sung by a sobbing confidant.
It caused light to drive though darkness.

Shadows filled the river;
The chimes of dispersing dreams
Rang out across the night,
The long wandering light searching
Through the water.
In the dark a boat was late in arriving.

Swimming across the purple waters was an injured man
An exile in his own river, slipping into the evening shade.
In the dark he pushed deeper into the swelling waters.

In the dense fog he was like a quivering bathtub
Whirling in an unexpected storm.
The gust brought more color
Washing over the swimmer;
Purple erasing purple.

# A Bronze Statue of Benjamin Franklin

In the courtyard of Old City Hall in Boston
Stands a bronze statue
Of Benjamin Franklin.

I sit in a rattan chair in the garden
In reverent contemplation of busy Ben
Working a printing press
Or drafting the Declaration of Independence.

A veteran fighter against imperial Britain,
A scientist, inventor and writer,
But never one to ask for laurels for himself;

In his epitaph penned when he was young
He wrote: This is the Body of B. Franklin,
Printer.

# Ode to Plane Trees

The plane trees glitter like gold,
Painting a long gallery:
Somewhere inside is the waning heart of autumn
Being shot into the distance on a celestial arrow.
Above them the mountains are shrouded in a fog
Which thinly veils a hamlet in a hollow;
A citron tree stands outside the hamlet,
Ripe fruits drroping from its branches
Like mother's milk-filled breasts.
Mother sits in a bamboo chair under the tree
Tearing off strands of her long hair
To mend the tears in my clothes;
Those threads
Are longer than the mountain trail,
A winding path of memories and longing.
The long gallery needs no tea hut for tired travelers;
The far mountains are shrouded in a fog
And the fog enfolds a sun.

# To My Nanny

Beside my warm, engulfing pillow,

I keep your small, faint smile.

It is hidden beyond sight, where

No one will yet find it.


It is a snapshot kept in an innocent mind.

I had no knowledge of love then,

Snug against your warm bosom,

Feeding on your light murmurs and your spring of milk.


When I left home and for the sea,

A trail of footprints was left in the sand.

Your smile floats into sight,

The moment I take each first step.

# Summer Rain

The footsteps of summer rain are tender and cool
Dancing across my bare chest.
Only the slender toes of young girls
Are as light and gentle…

What? Are these runaways?
The rain has become a gaggle of young girls,
Flitting about in terror. Look!
Their pursuer is catching up with his thunderous curses,
Brandishing a flexing whip.
Is he their father or a cruel master?
What crime have these girls committed?

Their almond eyes well with tears,

As they send their prayers into the distance.

I can hear the rustle of the gossamer hems of their skirts

Brushing against the flowering ground.

The trees curl down to help them hide.


What is the cause of this?

I shake my head free from these strange dreams.

Perhaps these girls are running in the high pavilions
    of clouds.

Ask the wind, that old uncouth wanderer,

For no place is off limits to him.

# Pursuit

After a pointless pursuit
I realize you have transcended distance.
So I have slipped through time
To open a hidden door into your life,
To find myself in your reflection.

Distance is the beginning of forgetting.
Clouds of red birds feast on the sun;
My pursuit of you shall be rewarded
When I have stolen time's long cloak.

# Postscript

Early this year we were asked by the Shanghai Writers' Association to put together an anthology of poems, to be called "Voices from the Sea", as a showcase of the work of Shanghai poets in recent years. It was to be translated into English to facilitate literary exchange. Shanghai boasts many accomplished poets and we therefore decided to restrict the collection to works by members of the Shanghai Writers' Association.

After we agreed to undertake the project, we carried out discussions on the division of work. Sun Qin'an was given the job of making the initial selection of poems, while Yang Binhua was given the task of making adjustments and supplements. When issues arose, we would consult each other to reach a consensus.

Since there was limited space in the collection and we were working to a tight deadline, we decided to make our selection based solely on works and collections that were already available to us. In the process of selection we set out to ensure that the anthology would be broadly representative of a variety of different styles and movements, as well as different age groups. The contribution of each author was limited to a maximum of three poems.

Our work has been characterized by diligence and cooperation. While we have tried our best to make it a success, we ask for the indulgence of readers should they find any errors or omissions. We would appreciate any suggestions for corrections or improvement.

Sun Qin'an & Yang Binhua

21 July, 2007